GREAT TRIALS OF THE TWENTIETH CENTURY ™

THE TRIAL OF JULIUS AND ETHEL ROSENBERG

A Primary Source Account

Betty Burnett, Ph.D.

rosen central
Primary Source ™

The Rosen Publishing Group, Inc., New York

To Janet

Published in 2004 by The Rosen Publishing Group, Inc.
29 East 21st Street, New York, NY 10010

First Edition

Library of Congress Cataloging-in-Publication Data

Burnett, Betty, 1940–
The trial of Julius and Ethel Rosenberg : a primary source account/
by Betty Burnett.—1st ed.
    p. cm.—(Great trials of the twentieth century)
Includes bibliographical references and index.
ISBN 0-8239-3976-6 (library binding)
1. Rosenberg, Julius, 1918–1953—Trials, litigation, etc. 2. Rosenberg, Ethel, 1915–1953—Trials, litigation, etc. 3. Trials (Espionage)—New York (State)—New York. 4. Trials (Conspiracy)—New York (State)—New York.
I. Title. II. Series.
KF224.R6 B87 2003
345.73'0231—dc21

                                                    2002153353

Manufactured in the United States of America

Unless otherwise attributed, all quotes in this book are excerpted from court transcripts.

CONTENTS

Rosenberg demonstrators gather at New York City's Pennsylvania Station to travel to Washington, D.C., in this photograph taken June 18, 1953. In the nation's capital, they joined a rally protesting the death sentence of Julius and Ethel Rosenberg, convicted spies set to die in the electric chair. The husband and wife were granted a brief stay of execution by Supreme Court justice William Douglas and were supported with demonstrations around the world.

INTRODUCTION

Ethel and Julius Rosenberg were the only American citizens ever put to death for spying on the United States for a foreign nation during peacetime. They were charged with conspiring to give military secrets to the Soviet Union in 1945, during the last year of World War II. At that time, the Soviet Union was an ally. Six years later, at the time of the Rosenbergs' trial, the Soviet Union was America's greatest enemy.

The Rosenbergs claimed that they were innocent until the moment they died. Many Americans still believe that they were not guilty. On the other hand, the Rosenbergs offered no hard evidence—only their own testimony—in their defense. In addition, a half dozen admitted spies testified against them.

Questions about the trial remain today. Was it fair? Was their punishment too harsh? What was really on trial: the Rosenbergs or communism? Were they punished for what they believed or for what they did?

The trial took place in 1951, shortly after the Cold War (1945–1991) began between the United States and the Soviet Union, and during the Korean War (1950–1953). Communist North Korea

President Harry S. Truman is shown signing a proclamation declaring a state of national emergency, in this photo taken at his desk in the White House in Washington, D.C., on December 16, 1950. The president was responding to the November 6 entry of Communist China into the Korean conflict.

invaded South Korea in 1950, and the United States joined the war on the side of South Korea. Americans were afraid of Communist expansion and aggression. They feared that if Communism spread throughout the world, they would lose democracy and freedom. After giving up so much to keep democracy and freedom during World War II (1941–1945), they were angry that they had to fight another war.

This fear and anger against Communism, known now as the Red Scare, turned the Rosenberg trial into a major event. The Rosenbergs became symbols of the hated Communists. Even worse, they had enjoyed all the benefits of American citizenship, and then, so it seemed, they betrayed their own country. Very few Americans came to the Rosenbergs' defense during their trial, but afterward, when their anger cooled, the questions began.

WHO WERE THE ROSENBERGS?

CHAPTER 1

Putting together the story of the Rosenberg trial is like putting together a jigsaw puzzle. There are many different pieces and at first it looks like they won't fit together. Some of the people involved had been friends for many years; others didn't know each other except by code names; and four were related to each other, either by blood or by marriage.

Spying, or espionage, is a federal crime in the United States, so a federal agency, the Federal Bureau of Investigation (FBI), did the detective work that caught the Rosenbergs. The local and state police were not involved.

The story started in the early years of World War II, when a partially burned codebook belonging to the KGB, the Soviet secret police, was found on a battlefield in Finland. As British and American code breakers figured out the secret messages in the book, they learned that a spy ring was operating in North America. Canadian and American citizens were giving military secrets to Soviet officials.

In the United States, the FBI began investigating the spy ring. They uncovered two names: Max Elitcher, who was employed by the U.S.

During the Cold War, when they were bitter enemies, the United States government devoted much of its time to spying on the Soviet Union. This Associated Press photograph, taken on April 24, 1956, shows Soviet authorities discovering a tunnel filled with surveillance equipment in Berlin, Germany. The Soviet Union claimed the United States had dug the tunnel and used the equipment to tap Russian telephone lines.

Navy's weapons department, and Joel Barr, an engineer who was working on radar systems. Since the FBI could find no proof that these men were spies, they dropped the investigation. The Allies were winning the war at that time, and it didn't seem as if spies could do any damage.

Then, in the summer of 1949, four years after World War II ended, the FBI found some papers from the Soviet consulate's office in New York City. One of the papers was an old coded report on the progress of the Manhattan Project from 1944. This top-secret government project was created by the Allies to make an atomic bomb. The British atomic scientist Klaus Fuchs had written the report. Had he given the report to the Soviets or did they steal it from him?

The FBI turned this information over to the authorities in Great Britain. A spy catcher went to Fuchs's office to question him. To everyone's surprise, Fuchs didn't try to hide anything. He quickly admitted to giving information to the Soviets while he worked on the atomic bomb in the United States, and he said his contact in New York was a man named Raymond.

Back in the United States, the FBI wanted to know more. Who was Raymond? Fuchs described him as a thirty-year-old man, who stood five feet eight inches tall, and was stocky, with dark, prematurely thinning hair. Fuchs didn't know his last name. That wasn't much to go on, but the FBI kept digging.

Klaus Emil Fuchs (circled) confessed to passing secrets about the Manhattan Project to the Soviets. In the above photograph, taken in 1959, Fuchs is escorted from Heathrow Airport in London, England. The atomic scientist indirectly led authorities to Julius Rosenberg. Although sentenced to fourteen years in a British prison, Fuchs served only nine. He died on January 28, 1988, at the age of seventy-six.

After a few months, FBI agents discovered that "Raymond" was really the Swiss-born Harry Gold, a chemist who worked for a New York engineering firm. The FBI picked up Gold, who admitted to being a courier, a person who took messages from spies to Soviet officials. Gold told the FBI agents that he took information about the atomic bomb from a soldier at Los Alamos, New Mexico, and passed it on to Anatoli A. Yakovlev, the Soviet vice consul in New York City.

Anatoli A. Yakovlev

Julius Rosenberg

Harry Gold

Morton Sobell

David Greenglass

Klaus Fuchs

Now there was a new link in the spy ring. Harry Gold didn't know the soldier's name, but he knew where he had lived on High Street in Albuquerque in June 1945. He described the soldier as being about twenty-five years old, and five feet seven inches tall, with dark brown curly hair, a snub nose, and a wide mouth. Gold added that he thought the soldier's wife's name was Ruth.

The FBI had to identify this soldier from the hundreds who had been stationed at Los Alamos at that time. A curious coincidence made their job easy. In 1950, the FBI was investigating the theft of small amounts of uranium from Manhattan Project labs in Los Alamos. Some soldiers had taken the uranium as souvenirs. When agents looked through the list of those working in Los Alamos, they found a man whose address was High Street, matching the address Gold gave of his contact there. This man was identified as David Greenglass. His wife's name was Ruth. Agents showed Gold a picture of Greenglass and the house in Albuquerque. He didn't remember Greenglass exactly, but he was sure of the house.

The FBI quickly found Greenglass in New York City in June 1950, and called him in for questioning. Like Fuchs and Gold, Greenglass was ready to talk. Yes, he had given information to Gold about the atomic bomb. Why? Because his brother-in-law had asked him to. His brother-in-law's name was Julius Rosenberg. Julius was married to David's sister, Ethel.

This chart shows part of the Soviet spy ring Julius Rosenberg was allegedly involved in. Anatoli Yakovlev was head of the Russian UN delegation and the KGB's chief of U.S. spy operations. According to Harry Gold, Yakovlev gave him David Greenglass's name and address. Gold was given information about the bomb by Klaus Fuchs. Greenglass was Julius Rosenberg's brother-in-law. Morton Sobell was an old friend of Rosenberg's.

The love felt between Julius and Ethel Rosenberg was rivaled only by their political ideals. After meeting at a New Year's Eve party, the two fell in love immediately and became inseparable. It was torture for them to be housed in separate prisons, and their love letters during their confinement show great passion and tenderness.

THE ROSENBERGS

Julius Rosenberg was born in 1918 and grew up in a Jewish neighborhood on the Lower East Side of Manhattan. Julius's father worked in the garment industry. As a boy, Julius loved to study and was very interested in ideas, especially ideas about justice. As many of the people around him, Julius was drawn to the idea of socialism. Under socialism, the state or government owns everything, including stores and factories. All workers are paid similar salaries by the state.

When Julius learned about communism, it seemed even better to him than socialism. In an ideal communistic society, everyone would be treated the same, no matter their race, religion, or social status. Communists believed there wouldn't be any very rich people who hogged resources or very poor people without anything. Everyone would have an equal piece of the pie.

After graduating from high school in 1933, Julius decided to be an electrical engineer. He attended City College of New York (CCNY), where political ideas were in the air, especially those considered left-wing—socialism and communism. The United States was in the midst of the Great Depression. Many workers had lost their jobs. Julius thought that if the U.S. government became communist, there would be no more depressions, and no one would ever lose a job again.

At CCNY, Julius met Max Elitcher, William Perl, Morton Sobell, and Joel Barr, fellow engineering students who shared his political views. He also met a young woman named Ethel Greenglass. Ethel was born in 1915, into the same Jewish neighborhood on the Lower East Side of Manhattan as Julius. As a girl, Ethel wanted to be an actress and a singer. She was the leading lady in most of her school plays. She was also very smart and studied hard for her classes. Her hard work paid off. She skipped two grades and graduated from high school when she was only fifteen. She didn't care about going to college. She was ready to go to work.

Ethel began looking for a job in 1930, at the beginning of the Great Depression when jobs were scarce. Businesses were laying off workers, not hiring new ones. Ethel kept pushing and found a job as a shipping clerk. After four years, she became upset with working conditions at her job. She convinced 150 of her coworkers to go on strike. They stopped working and lay down in the middle of the street so the company's trucks couldn't get out to make their deliveries. Ethel thought working conditions would be better and more stable under a communist system of government.

Julius and Ethel met at a New Year's Eve dance where she was singing. They married in 1939 and moved to a small apartment in Brooklyn. By 1940, Julius found a good job as an inspector of electronic equipment for the U.S. Army Signal Corps. He was a civilian employee, meaning that he never joined the army. Both Julius and Ethel were active members of the Communist Party for a few years. Some historians believe that they dropped out so that they wouldn't be suspected of spying.

The Rosenbergs had two sons. Michael was born in 1943, and Robert was born in 1947. The Rosenbergs were an ordinary family who lived in an ordinary apartment complex. There was nothing about them that was unusual or that attracted anyone's attention.

In this photograph taken on June 10, 1953, in Washington, D.C., ten-year-old Michael Rosenberg *(right)* puts his arm around his six-year-old brother, Robert. At the time of this picture, the boys' parents were making their fourth plea to the Supreme Court to escape death by the electric chair. Witnesses to their father's arrest, the boys marched on behalf of their parents, carrying signs that read, "Don't Kill My Mommy and Daddy."

David Greenglass, Ethel's younger brother, grew up admiring his sister's boyfriend. He frequently said that Julius was his idol. They often sat around the kitchen table with Ethel until late at night discussing their favorite subject—politics. David was a passionate communist and so was his girlfriend, Ruth Abel. Both were members of the Young Communist League, just as Julius and Ethel had been.

Being a member of the Communist Party was not against the law then. The way Americans saw communism in the 1930s was very different from how it was seen in the 1950s, when most Americans hated it. Many students, artists, writers, scientists, labor leaders, and people in the theater were interested in communism, both as a form of government and an economic system. Many Americans thought communism was working very well in the Soviet Union, under the leadership of Joseph Stalin. This is partially because only good news about communism was allowed to leave the Soviet Union. All the bad news was kept secret. It seemed as if Jews were treated better in the Soviet Union than they were in the United States.

The truth was that many Jews were treated much worse in the Soviet Union than in the United States. Some were even imprisoned and

Taken on November 3, 1932, in New York City, this photograph shows a rally for the Socialist Party held in Madison Square Garden. Twenty-two thousand socialist supporters listened to the words of socialist presidential candidate Norman Thomas, who ran unsuccessfully six times.

killed. Many artists and intellectuals wanted to leave the Soviet Union and move to the United States. Many of them were also imprisoned, tortured, and killed. Joseph Stalin was a cruel dictator despite his image as a friendly "Uncle Joe." Americans didn't find out about Stalin's death camps, where he put those who opposed him, until the 1950s.

In the 1930s, it was not unusual for people who wanted to end poverty and injustice to think of helping the Soviets spread communism. They thought they were working to make the world a better place.

THE ARRESTS

Early on the morning of June 16, 1950, a few days after David Greenglass had been arrested for espionage, FBI agents knocked on the Rosenbergs' door. Julius agreed to go downtown to talk with the agents as soon as he finished shaving. He didn't allow them to search the apartment without a search warrant.

According to the book *The Rosenberg Files*, by Ronald Radosh and Joyce Milton, one agent asked, "What would you say if we told you your brother-in-law said you asked him to supply information for the Russians?"

"Bring him here," Julius replied. "I'll call him a liar to his face."

After a few hours of questioning, Julius was released without being arrested. Meanwhile, the FBI continued to gather evidence against him. A few evenings later, there was another knock on the Rosenbergs' apartment door. When Julius opened the door, the agents clapped handcuffs onto him and took him away while his young sons watched. This time the FBI had a warrant for his arrest and a search warrant for his apartment. They collected all the papers they could find and took

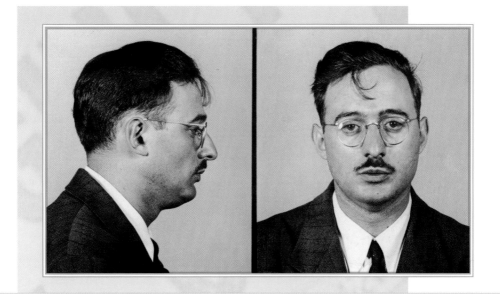

Arrested on July 17, 1950, Julius Rosenberg was never to return home in the years before he was executed, on June 19, 1953. Although evidence against Ethel was scant, the FBI arrested her in hopes that her husband would confess to spying for the Soviets. When Julius didn't sway from his story of innocence, the government was forced to continue prosecuting Ethel as a partner in the conspiracy.

them to the FBI office. Ethel was not arrested. She was allowed to stay home with her children.

Thousands of miles away that same week in June, North Korean forces invaded South Korea. North Korea was a Communist nation, backed by the Soviet Union. President Harry S. Truman promised to help South Korea fight Communism. The news about Korea appeared alongside the Rosenberg story on the front pages of newspapers across the nation. The suspected communist spy Julius Rosenberg immediately lost any sympathy he might have had.

THE GRAND JURY

While Julius was in jail, the FBI continued to gather evidence for a grand jury. The grand jury system is a way of protecting people accused

FBI agents escort Julius Rosenberg into the FBI building in New York City in this photograph taken on July 17, 1950. **Inset:** A photographic portrait of Morton Sobell, who was tried with the Rosenbergs. Living in Mexico with his wife and children at the time of Julius Rosenberg's arrest, Sobell was kidnapped by Mexican thugs and taken to the U.S. border, where he was arrested for conspiracy to commit espionage. The photograph is housed in the United States National Archives.

of certain crimes, including federal crimes. Espionage (or spying) is a capital crime as well as a federal crime, one that can be punished with death. The U.S. Constitution states that no one shall be tried for a capital crime without an indictment (formal accusation) from a grand jury—twelve people who sit in judgment and decide whether there is enough evidence to warrant a trial. This is to ensure that people will not be publicly accused of serious crimes without probable cause.

Testimony given to a grand jury is kept secret in case there is no indictment. It is not made public as it is in a trial. When a grand jury decides that enough evidence exists to warrant holding a public trial, it writes a "true bill." If it decides there's not enough evidence, it reports a "no bill."

The grand jury hearing for Julius Rosenberg was set for August 8, 1950. Ethel was called to testify, as well as Harry Gold and others. After testifying, Ethel left the courtroom and went to the subway station to go home. FBI agents followed her, and before she could get on the train, they insisted that she return with them. There they arrested her and expanded the grand jury hearing to include her, as well as Julius. The grand jury returned a true bill for both of the Rosenbergs, and they never returned home. Another man was also indicted with them. He was Morton Sobell, a friend of Julius Rosenberg's from CCNY.

THE INDICTMENT

The Rosenbergs and Sobell were charged with conspiracy to commit espionage, not espionage itself. "Conspiracy" is defined as an agreement among two or more people to do something illegal or criminal at any level of government—county, state, or national. Proving conspiracy is easier than proving other crimes, such as treason or murder. Hearsay testimony—something a witness heard someone else say about a defendant—is allowed. It is not necessary to prove conspirators actually succeeded in their plans to commit a crime, only that they conspired together to plan an illegal act.

Once the existence of a conspiracy has been established, each conspirator may be held liable (legally responsible) for the acts of all the others, whether or not he or she had specific knowledge of the acts. So if David Greenglass, his wife Ruth, his sister Ethel, and her husband Julius talked about spying and only David actually spied, they all would be considered guilty of the act.

TREASON

The Rosenbergs were not charged with treason, although many people think they were. Article III, Section 3, of the U.S. Constitution states, "Treason against the United States shall consist only in levying war against them, or in adhering to their enemies, giving them aid and comfort." During the twentieth century, the meaning of treason was expanded to mean "a criminal offense involving the attempt, by overt acts, to overthrow the government to which the offender owes allegiance or to betray the state to a foreign power."

Treason is a very difficult crime to prove.

The legal definition of espionage includes transmitting information "relating to the national defense to the advantage of a foreign nation." The key word is "foreign" nation. It doesn't matter if the nation is an ally or an enemy.

The Rosenberg-Sobell trial was set for March 1951. Both sides, the prosecution and the defense, needed the six months to prepare their cases. They had to interview dozens of witnesses and gather information on what the Rosenbergs and Greenglasses did during the 1940s, who they saw, and where they went. The prosecutors had to connect the Rosenbergs and Sobell with known spies and show that they had the opportunity to get information to the Soviets. The defense attorneys had to find enough information to show that it was impossible for the Rosenbergs to have spied during that period.

The judge for the trial was Irving R. Kaufman. He had a reputation for being very tough and also very smart.

THE JURY

Before the trial could begin, a jury had to be selected. Both the defense and the prosecution have the right to question jurors and to accept or reject them. As a group, the potential jurors for the Rosenberg trial were asked a series of questions: Did they have definite feelings about communism, for instance, or about the atomic bomb? Did they read communist magazines or anticommunist newspapers? Did any of their family members work for the FBI or in law enforcement?

Jurors have to promise that they will give the defendants a fair trial. Judge Kaufman told the panel that "the minds of the jurors should be the same as a white sheet of paper with nothing on it, with respect to this case, and you only take the testimony as it comes from the witnesses and from no other source."

Some people could not promise to be unbiased; they were excused from serving on the jury. Many people who had served in the military during World War II or who had lost relatives in the war had strong feelings about serving their country and did not believe that they could consider a case fairly that dealt with spying for the enemy. Some who had friends or relatives headed for the war in Korea were prejudiced against people charged with spying.

After several days of questioning, the final twelve jurors were chosen. They included two accountants, a bookkeeper, a restaurant owner,

This photograph, taken outside Federal Court in New York City on March 29, 1951, shows the jury for the Rosenberg spy trial. Jurors took very little time to decide a guilty verdict for all three defendants. Foreman Vincent LeBonette stands center, holding his hat. None of the jurors were Jewish, and only one, Lisette Dammas, was female.

a housewife, a store manager, a caterer for a tennis club, an electrical company worker, two auditors, a secretary, and an estimator. There was one woman and one African American. The rest were white men.

The judge told the jury, "I admonish you now . . . not to discuss [the case] with our fellow jurors, not to discuss it with anybody at home, not to permit anybody to discuss the case with you, and of course, not to read a newspaper, read anything in a newspaper concerning this case, not to listen to the radio, not to watch television, and at no time to read any magazine that deals with this particular case."

Although the jurors might not hear the news in the coming weeks, they could not erase the memories of what they had lived through. Their minds could never be "a blank sheet of paper." Everything they had heard or seen about World War II was still in their minds, and they couldn't escape the nervousness that all Americans felt about atomic weapons.

THE ATOMIC BOMB

The year 1942 was very dark for the United States. The attack on the U.S. naval base at Pearl Harbor, Hawaii, had brought the country into World War II in December 1941. Americans were not prepared to go to war; many did not want to get involved with the troubles in Europe and Asia that had been brewing for many years. The army and navy were using equipment that was twenty years old. There weren't enough uniforms, weapons, airplanes, tanks, or bandages to fight a war.

In Europe, the Nazis occupied France, Belgium, and the Netherlands. They were bombing England, and they were marching into Soviet territory. Both the British and the Soviet people were bravely fighting back, but they needed help badly. On the Pacific front, Japan was winning battle after battle. It was impossible for Americans to believe, but it seemed like the war would be lost.

The United States needed a weapon so powerful it could win the war quickly. As more and more German and eastern European scientists fled to the United States as refugees, rumors of a secret Nazi weapon involving atomic energy began to surface. This frightened many Americans. The U.S. government brought atomic scientists, chemists, and physicists together to pool their brainpower. America would build an atomic bomb, too, and America would build it first.

THE MANHATTAN PROJECT

Even before the United States entered World War II in 1941, scientists were considering building a bomb powered by fission, a form of

In this photograph, taken on February 18, 1955, U.S. soldiers watch an atomic bomb test in Yucca Flat, Nevada. After dropping atomic bombs on Hiroshima and Nagasaki, Japan, during World War II, the United States conducted test explosions in locations in the Pacific Ocean and in Nevada. Testing started in Yucca Flat in 1951 and was halted in 1958, but it was resumed in 1961. It continues today.

atomic energy. By 1942, several lines of atomic research were carried on at the same time in the race to get the bomb built. This enormous project was conducted in facilities throughout the United States, from New York City (where the project was given its code name "Manhattan") to Washington State to the University of Chicago to the desert of New Mexico. Scientists from Great Britain came to the United States, bringing their knowledge and expertise. One of them was Klaus Fuchs.

The elements used for the atomic bomb (A-bomb) were uranium and plutonium. These elements were developed into pure metals and then shaped into bomb components at a laboratory in Los Alamos, New Mexico, near Albuquerque.

A machinist named David Greenglass was one of many U.S. soldiers assigned to the A-bomb project at Los Alamos. He became the assistant foreman in the theta shop, the high explosives unit. There he learned about detonating the bomb. The bomb was going to implode, rather than explode as did other weapons of its kind. In an explosion such as that caused by dynamite, shock waves travel outward. The force is so great, it knocks down whatever is in its path, whether it is a person, a car, or a building. In an implosion, the energy turns inward, concentrating itself into a critical mass. Then it explodes with many times the power of dynamite, creating a fireball that vaporizes everything in its path.

The detonation device for this implosion was called a lens, although it was nothing like an ordinary glass lens. It was cast in a mold in the theta shop, where David Greenglass was the foreman. Several slightly different implosion lenses were designed before the final version was accepted. All these were drawn up in sketches.

In the summer of 1945, all the parts of the atomic bomb were assembled at Los Alamos. The bomb was test-detonated 120 miles south of Albuquerque early on the morning of July 16. There was an intense

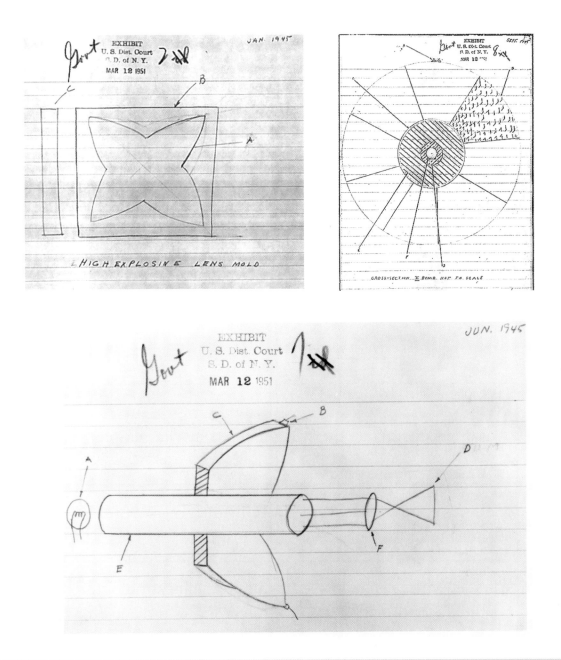

Drawn by Ethel Rosenberg's brother, David Greenglass, these sketches were entered into court as exhibits in the Rosenberg trial. The high explosive lens mold from the atomic bomb *(top left)* was government exhibit 2 and was drawn in January 1945. Government exhibit 8 *(top right)* shows a cross section of the atomic bomb. The defense successfully argued that this sketch should be kept secret from everyone, so the jury never saw it. The bottom diagram, government exhibit 7, is a sketch of a setup to implode tubular materials. All sketches are from the Julius and Ethel Rosenberg Case File (1951) and are now housed in the National Archives Record Administration.

THE SOVIET UNION VS. THE UNITED STATES IN 1951

SOVIET UNION	UNITED STATES
Rule by command (totalitarianism)	Rule by representatives elected by the people (democracy)
Collective (government) ownership of property	Individual ownership of property
Shelter, education, and medical care provided for all by the government	Shelter, education, and medical care provided for those in need by community organizations (schools and hospitals), local governments, and some state agencies
Belief in controlling other nations by force	Belief in creating alliances among nations

flash of light, a sudden wave of heat, and a tremendous roar as a fireball ignited, followed by its trademark, a mushroom cloud that rose 40,000 feet into the air, spreading dangerous radioactivity. The test was a success, and the bomb was used three weeks later on Japan at Hiroshima and Nagasaki, ending the war.

American scientists and military leaders knew this A-bomb was the most powerful, most dangerous weapon on Earth. They didn't want any other nation on Earth to have one, particularly not an enemy. Some nations, on the other hand, wanted the secret of the A-bomb very badly. The Soviet Union was one.

After World War II, the Soviets began building their own atomic bomb. They successfully detonated one in August 1949. This made the American military very nervous. It was clear by then that Joseph Stalin was going to keep all the land that had

An atomic bomb explodes into a fiery mushroom cloud in this photograph taken on March 27, 1954. This test detonation, code-named "Romeo," was conducted over the Bikini Atoll, a popular site for atomic testing in the central Pacific's Marshall Islands.

been occupied by Soviet troops during the war—Poland, Hungary, Bulgaria, Albania, Lithuania, and other small countries. These new Soviet satellites, known as the Eastern Bloc were said to be behind an Iron Curtain that kept them imprisoned. All together, the countries of the Soviet Union and the Eastern Bloc seemed powerful enough to take over the rest of the world, and now they had an A-bomb.

These photographs, taken in New York City on May 19, 1955, advertise a packaged fallout shelter marketed by Walter Kiddie Nuclear Laboratories, Inc., to families concerned about the potential effects of the atomic bomb on their lives. Many families in the 1950s purchased such shelters with the intention of fleeing to a safe house in the event of nuclear war. The unit shown in the pictures was supposed to be able to protect a family from radiation and sustain them for three to five days.

As fear of the Soviet Union took hold of America, families thought about stockpiling food and water in case of an attack. Some even built bomb shelters. Atom bomb drills were held in schools. Irving Saypol, the U.S. attorney who prosecuted the Rosenbergs, called the atom bomb "one weapon that might well hold the key to the survival of this nation." In 1951, a ghostly "mushroom cloud" seemed to be hanging over the world.

THE PROSECUTION

On March 6, 1951, the trial known as the *United States v. Julius Rosenberg, Ethel Rosenberg, David Greenglass, and Morton Sobell* began.

The U.S. legal system has established rules that must be followed during a trial; anyone who doesn't follow the rules is penalized. There may be surprises during the trial, but the rules cannot change once the trial begins. Certain rules for trying a crime committed locally may be different than those in a case involving a federal offense. Each jurisdiction—city, county, state, or nation—has its own set of rules that lawyers, judges, and juries must follow.

Like all U.S. trials, the Rosenbergs' trial followed a strict procedure of rules set up in the U.S. Constitution. The Constitution states that all accused persons are assumed innocent until the "burden of proof" shows that they are guilty beyond a reasonable doubt. Prosecutors assume the burden of proof. They must persuade a jury that the defendant is guilty by showing them physical evidence and by calling for testimony relevant to the crime. Beyond a "reasonable"

In this photograph taken on April 19, 1950, in New York City, U.S. attorney Irving Saypol *(left)* hands letters of appointment to chief assistant U.S. attorney Myles Lane *(center)* and Roy Cohn *(right)*, assistant to the U.S. attorney. Saypol was the chief prosecutor in the Rosenberg trial and served as a mentor to Cohn, who went on to become notorious for his overzealous tactics to root out all communists in America while he worked as an aide to Senator Joseph McCarthy.

doubt doesn't mean that there isn't any doubt. It means that an average person would find conviction of the defendant logical and necessary.

The chief prosecutor in the Rosenberg trial was U.S. attorney Irving Saypol. He was called a "Red hunter" because he spent much of his time looking for communists. He made no secret of the fact that he hated communism. In his opening statement, Saypol said, "The evidence will show that the loyalty and the allegiance of the Rosenbergs . . . was to Communism" and not to the United States.

Defense attorney Emanuel (Manny) Bloch objected, saying, "Communism is not on trial here." Although the judge agreed, Saypol continued to talk about communism with scorn.

THE STRATEGY

The prosecutor sets the stage for a trial with an opening statement that outlines the government's case against the defendant. Evidence is gradually presented to back up what the prosecutor says.

The case against the Rosenbergs was based primarily on the testimony of others who were involved in the spy ring. Often, testimony alone is not enough to convict someone of a crime because memories are selective. Witnesses may forget certain important words, or they may have looked away when something crucial was happening. They usually remember only what seems important to them. For this reason, attorneys must keep asking them questions.

Witnesses must swear that their testimony is true. Although some may still lie, they are less likely to lie under oath because if they are caught, they are guilty of perjury and can be fined or sent to jail.

THE TESTIMONY: MAX ELITCHER

The first witness called by the prosecution was Max Elitcher. Elitcher, an old friend of both Sobell and Julius Rosenberg, had already confessed to being a spy. First, he testified against Sobell. Then the prosecutor asked Elitcher if Julius Rosenberg had visited him in Washington D.C., while he was working for the navy. He replied,

Yes, he called me and reminded me of our school friendship and came to my home . . . Then he began talking about the job that the Soviet Union was doing in the war effort and how a good deal of military information was being denied them by some interests in the United States . . . He said there were many people who were implementing aid to the Soviet Union by providing classified information about military equipment and asked whether in my capacity at the Bureau of Ordnance working on anti-aircraft devices, and computer control of firing missiles, would I turn information over to him? He told me that any information I gave him would be taken to New York, processed photographically and would be returned overnight—so it would not be missed.

This photograph of David and Ruth Greenglass was exhibit 13 of the Julius and Ethel Rosenberg Case File (1951). It is housed in the National Archives. In Sam Roberts's 2001 biography, *The Brother*, Greenglass admitted that he committed perjury during the Rosenberg trial, dooming his sister to die in the electric chair.

This testimony established a link between Julius Rosenberg and Elitcher, who had already confessed to spying.

DAVID AND RUTH GREENGLASS

Both David and Ruth Greenglass told the FBI and the grand jury everything they knew about everyone they knew. They held nothing back. From the beginning, they cooperated with the authorities and seemed to be telling the truth. On the witness stand, under Saypol's questioning, they told their story for the jury. Several parts of their story incriminated the Rosenbergs.

According to David, in January 1945, while he was still in the army, he was given a furlough (vacation) from the Los Alamos laboratory.

Entered into evidence as government exhibit 3, this photograph of Mike and Ann Sidorovich was part of the Julius and Ethel Rosenberg Case File (1951) and is now in the National Archives Records Administration. Ann Sidorovich was to be the transporter of information between David Greenglass and Julius Rosenberg. David Greenglass testified that Sidorovich would obtain information from Greenglass in a Denver, Colorado, movie theater, and take it to New York City. In her testimony, Ethel Rosenberg denied any such plan.

Ruth was living in Albuquerque then. The couple went to New York for a week. One evening they went to the Rosenbergs' for dinner. They met another guest there, Ann Sidorovich of Cleveland, Ohio. Julius told them that Ann would be the courier bringing information from the Greenglasses in New Mexico to New York.

This photograph of the Jell-O box entered into evidence as government exhibit 33 was to serve as a representative of the box allegedly cut by Julius Rosenberg and given to Ruth Greenglass as an identifier. It is part of the Julius and Ethel Rosenberg Case File (1951) and is housed in the National Archives Records Administration.

After dinner, Julius asked Ruth to go into the kitchen with him so that he could give her a recognition signal, to be used in case Ann Sidorovich couldn't go and another courier had to be sent in her place. Recognition signals are words or objects that only those involved in the spy ring would know.

Julius took a Jell-O box from the kitchen cabinet, emptied the contents, and cut the side panel of the box into two irregularly shaped pieces. He kept one and gave the other to Ruth, who took it into the living room to show David. When the courier met them in New Mexico, he or she would have the other piece of the box.

Another major point in the Greenglasses' testimonies was about a mahogany console table in the Rosenbergs' living room. The Greenglasses said that it came from the Soviets and was used for photographing secret documents onto microfilm.

David Greenglass admitted that he had drawn a sketch of the lens for the atomic bomb and a sketch of the spherical lens mold design, and supplied a description of plutonium reductions experiments. Atomic scientists testified that it was part of the bomb. Greenglass then said that he had given the sketch to Julius to be photographed.

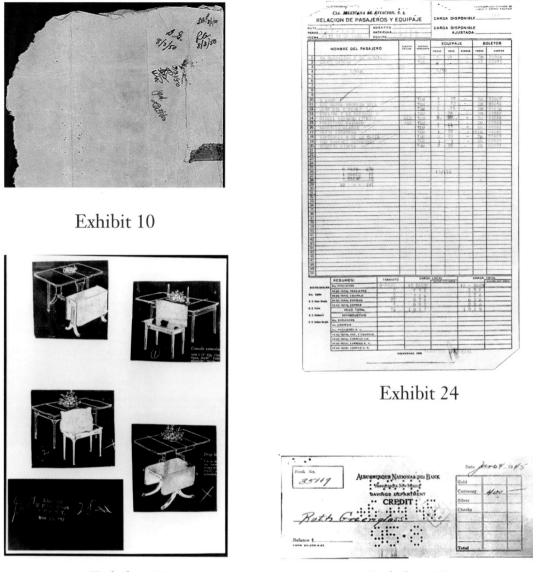

Exhibit 10

Exhibit 24

Exhibit 28

Exhibit 17

Shown above are documents entered into evidence in the Rosenberg trial. **Exhibit 10:** brown paper wrapper which contained $4,000 that Julius Rosenberg gave to David Greenglass in 1950 with instructions to flee to Czechoslovakia. **Exhibit 24:** airline passenger manifests bearing the name N. Sand, an alias used by Morton Sobell. **Exhibit 28:** Photostat of a console table similar to one owned by the Rosenbergs, which the Greenglasses claimed was for microfilming stolen documents. **Exhibit 17:** Bank deposit slip and ledger for the account of Ruth Greenglass from June 4, 1945, showing that David Greenglass had deposited $400 after Harry Gold's visit. All are part of the Julius and Ethel Rosenberg Case File (1951) and are housed in the National Archives Records Administration.

The Trial of Julius and Ethel Rosenberg

Ruth Greenglass claimed that Ethel Rosenberg typed up David's notes. Ruth's testimony strengthened the argument that Ethel was a conspirator with Julius and that she knew as much as he did.

HARRY GOLD

Harry Gold was brought to the trial from prison, where he was serving a thirty-year sentence for espionage after confessing to being a

This photograph, taken in Washington, D.C., on April 26, 1956, shows Rosenberg colleague Harry Gold (*right*) testifying at an open hearing of the Senate Internal Security Committee. Gold testified while he was imprisoned at the Lewisburg, Pennsylvania, federal penitentiary for his role in the Rosenberg spy case. The hearing was held to investigate the use of U.S. citizens by Soviet intelligence.

Soviet agent. At the Rosenberg trial, Gold said he worked as a courier for Anatoli Yakovlev, whose code name was "John." Yakovlev instructed him to get information from the New Mexico laboratory about the use of nuclear fission in the production of a military weapon.

Gold explained that he always used a recognition signal to be sure he was meeting up with the right people. In the spring of 1945, Gold met Yakovlev in a New York City restaurant. Yakovlev took an onion-skin paper from his pocket. On it was typed, "Greenglass, 259 North High Street." Underneath were the words, "I come from Julius." Yakovlev then took a piece of cardboard from another pocket. It was part of a Jell-O box, oddly cut.

"Show this to Greenglass. He will show you the other matching piece. Then you will be sure," Yakovlev said.

Gold traveled to New Mexico, where he found David and Ruth Greenglass. He told them, "I come from Julius." Then he gave them the piece from the Jell-O box. David and Ruth gave him the sketch of the implosion lens and a few pages of notes about how it would work.

After these major witnesses appeared, other witnesses were called to testify as well. Each of them held a piece of the puzzle and gave a little more information about the spy ring. The jury listened to them all and waited for the defense to begin.

THE DEFENSE

Defense attorneys must use all their knowledge and skill to fight for their clients. No matter what the prosecutor, judge, other witnesses, or the media says about them, they must keep focused on telling their client's story. In a criminal trial, a defense attorney's duty is to create a reasonable doubt in the minds of the jurors, as to the defendant's guilt. He or she should object to anything that breaks the rules of presenting evidence. In addition, he or she must cross-examine (question again) witnesses for the prosecution to be sure their testimony is all of the truth, not just a part of it.

Manny Bloch made the arguments for the defense of Julius Rosenberg. His father, Alexander Bloch, argued on behalf of Ethel. Morton Sobell's attorney was Edward Kuntz. The Blochs' defense strategy has been criticized for being too weak. Many lawyers who have since studied the trial transcripts claim that the Blochs missed many opportunities to object when the prosecution seemed to break a rule. The Blochs seemed timid in their defense, perhaps afraid that they would be called un-American or communist sympathizers.

Manny Bloch's opening statement to the jury asked them to be fair to Julius Rosenberg. ". . . All we ask of you is a fair shake in the American way. All we ask of you is to keep your minds open until all the evidence is in . . . We ask you to judge this defendant, an American citizen, as you would want to be judged yourself . . ."

Alexander Bloch emphasized the crime of David Greenglass in his opening statement. He said on behalf of Ethel Rosenberg: "You are not to condemn her because her brother is a self-confessed traitor."

The Rosenbergs' legal team leaves the U.S. Supreme Court building in Washington, D.C., on June 19, 1953. From left to right stand John Finerty, Malcolm Sharp, Emanuel Bloch, Fyke Farmer, and Daniel Marshall. Sharp, Farmer, and Marshall entered the Rosenberg case at the appeal stage and convinced Associate Justice William Douglas that they should receive a stay of execution until further investigation. In a dramatic turn, the Court was called back from summer recess and ruled against the Rosenbergs.

The defense attorneys cross-examined Max Elitcher, Harry Gold, Ruth and David Greenglass, and the other witnesses against the Rosenbergs, but they couldn't get them to change their stories.

TESTIMONY OF THE ROSENBERGS

The defense called only two witnesses, Ethel and Julius Rosenberg. To begin with, Manny Bloch wanted to show that Julius was a patriotic American, not someone who served Soviet masters:

> Bloch: Do you owe allegiance to any other country?
> Rosenberg: I do not.
> Bloch: Have you any divided allegiance?
> Rosenberg: I do not.
> Bloch: Would you fight for this country?
> Rosenberg: Yes, I will.

When Judge Kaufman asked him if he had ever belonged to a group that had discussed the system of government in the Soviet Union, Julius pled the Fifth Amendment and said, "I refuse to answer a question that might tend to incriminate me."

The Fifth Amendment to the Constitution guarantees that no one "shall be compelled in any criminal case to be a witness against himself." This means that the defendant does not have to answer questions that might make him or her look guilty. Ethel used the Fifth Amendment for most of the questions that were asked her, even ordinary questions that would not hurt her case.

When the Rosenbergs and their lawyers chose to use the Fifth Amendment instead of answering questions, it was a critical decision that hurt them. Americans asked each other, "If they have nothing to hide, why don't they answer?"

Many times they did answer the questions. Julius refuted Max Elitcher's testimony that he had asked Elitcher to spy, saying that he'd

Julius and Ethel Rosenberg stand together during their trial in this 1951 photograph, taken in New York City. The Rosenbergs were the only defense witnesses called to the stand, and each pleaded the Fifth Amendment whenever a question about their relations with the Communist Party arose. This strategy of silence likely hurt their chances, especially Ethel's, making it difficult for the jury to sympathize with them.

never done that. Both the Rosenbergs denied everything the Greenglasses said about them. They didn't know anything about a Jell-O box or a dinner party with Ann Sidorovich (who could not be found). They had bought the "microfilming" console at Macy's for $21. It didn't come from the Soviets, and they never used it for microfilming. Ethel did not type David's notes.

The question came up, "Why would David lie about his sister and her husband?" The Rosenbergs claimed that David was angry because they had started a business together, and it had failed. David had lost money and the Rosenbergs thought he wanted to get revenge. But if that was true, he was hurting himself as well as the Rosenbergs by his testimony, because he was certain to go to prison, too.

At the end of her questioning, Ethel declared, "I know I am not guilty . . ."

THE VERDICT AND THE SENTENCE

A lawyer's closing statement to the jury is an essential part of the trial. It sums up everything about the case that will help the jury make a decision.

In the closing statement for the defense, Bloch appealed to the emotions of the jury rather than to logic. The Rosenbergs are innocent, he said, and David Greenglass was "repulsive" for testifying against his own sister. "He is the lowest of the lowest animals that I have ever seen." It was clear that Ruth Greenglass has fooled the FBI, he said and added, "I do hope she won't be able to fool you."

Saypol also appealed to the jury's emotions in the prosecution's closing. "Imagine a wheel," he said. "In the center of the wheel, Rosenberg, reaching out like the tentacles of an octopus." He ended his speech with, "These defendants before you are party to an agreement to spy and steal from their own country, to serve the interests of a foreign power which today seeks to wipe us off the face of the earth. [The Soviet Union] would use . . . the information . . . from these traitors to destroy Americans and the people of the United

Nations . . . No defendants ever stood before the bar of American justice less deserving of sympathy than these . . ."

After the summations were complete, Judge Kaufman reminded the jury, "You cannot have justice unless you are ready to approach your task of determining the issues with your minds completely barren of prejudice or sympathy . . . The burden is on the Government to establish guilt beyond a reasonable doubt."

The jurors received the case just minutes before 5 PM on March 28, 1951. They decided to have an early dinner before they began deliberations. U.S. marshals escorted them to a nearby Italian restaurant, then back to the jury room around 6 PM.

The Rosenbergs and their lawyers were taken to the jail in the basement of the courthouse. They were too nervous to be hungry. They sat silent, waiting. The judge waited in his chambers and the prosecutor in his office. Each time the jury had a question, they all had to go back to the courtroom. This occurred at 8:10 PM, 9:43 PM, and 10:55 PM. All the questions were minor and easily answered. At midnight, the jury foreman reported that they were too tired to continue, so the judge let them take a recess until 10 AM the next morning. U.S. marshals took them to a nearby hotel to spend the night.

At 10 AM, they were all back in the jury room. Just an hour later, at 11 AM, they announced they had reached a verdict and filed back into the courtroom where Judge Kaufman, Morton Sobell, the Rosenbergs, and their lawyers were waiting. David Greenglass had struck a deal and was not waiting for a verdict. The clerk asked the foreman, "How say you?"

The foreman replied, "We the jury find Julius Rosenberg guilty as charged. We the jury find Ethel Rosenberg guilty as charged. We the jury find Morton Sobell guilty as charged."

This photograph, taken on April 11, 1951, in Ossining, New York, captures the arrival of Ethel Rosenberg, flanked by U.S. deputy marshals Antony H. Pavone *(left)* and Sarah Goldstein *(right)*, at Sing Sing Prison, where she would eventually die in the electric chair. Rosenberg was the first woman to be put to death by the U.S. government since Mary Surratt, who had a role in the assassination of Abraham Lincoln.

THE SENTENCE

The verdict and the sentencing are two different parts of a trial. In this case, which was tried under the Espionage Act of 1917, the jury decided the verdict and the judge decided the sentence. Judge Kaufman

The Rosenbergs' codefendant, Morton Sobell (*right*) is transferred to Alcatraz Prison in this 1952 photograph. Sobell was sentenced to thirty years in prison, although he served only about half that. In 1974, Sobell published a memoir called *Doing Time.*

told the Rosenbergs and their lawyers that he would give them their sentence on April 5, 1951, after he'd thought about it for a week.

On that date, the Rosenbergs again stood before the judge in the courtroom. Kaufman talked to them for a while about the seriousness of the crime. Then he read these words:

"The sentence of the Court upon Julius and Ethel Rosenberg is, for the crime for which you have been convicted, you are hereby sentenced to the punishment of death, and it is ordered upon some day within the week beginning with Monday, May 21, you shall be executed according to law."

Shock went through the courtroom. The lawyers objected and promised to appeal—to ask a higher court to change the decision.

David Greenglass was given a prison term of fifteen years. His sentence was much lighter because he had cooperated with the FBI. Ruth Greenglass was not charged with a crime. She was an "unindicted co-conspirator." Morton Sobell was given a sentence of thirty years.

After the sentencing, the Rosenbergs were taken to Sing Sing Prison in Ossining, New York, to await their execution in the electric chair. Meanwhile, their lawyers vowed to fight back.

IN JUDGE KAUFMAN'S WORDS...

An excerpt from Judge Kaufman's statement upon sentencing the Rosenbergs:

"Citizens of this country who betray their fellow-countrymen can be under none of the delusions about the benignity of Soviet power that they might have been prior to World War II. The nature of Russian terrorism is now self-evident . . . I consider your crime worse than murder . . . [I]n your case, I believe your conduct in putting into the hands of the Russians the A-bomb years before our best scientists predicted Russia would perfect the bomb has already caused, in my opinion, the Communist aggression in Korea, with the resultant casualties exceeding 50,000 and who knows but that millions more of innocent people may pay the price of your treason. Indeed, by your betrayal you undoubtedly have altered the course of history to the disadvantage of our country . . . Indeed the defendants Julius and Ethel Rosenberg placed their devotion to their cause above their own personal safety and were conscious that they were sacrificing their own children, should their misdeeds be detected—all of which did not deter them from pursuing their course. Love for their cause dominated their lives—it was even greater than their love for their children."

THE APPEALS

Court reporters write down every word uttered in a court of law. This material can later be reviewed if the lawyers for the losing side want to appeal (challenge) the verdict. Appeals are heard or read in appellate court by judges. The case is not retried; new arguments are not added. Judges merely review the trial transcript, and defense lawyers point out errors that the prosecution or judge made. Appellate judges look for errors of law, not errors of fact. That is, they want to be sure that the correct procedure was used.

The Blochs stated that there were three main reasons for the appeal of the Rosenberg case. First, the government failed to prove that the Rosenbergs had acted with intent to do harm to the vital interest of the United States. Second, David Greenglass testified against his sister and brother-in-law for personal reasons that had nothing to do with national security. Third, Judge Kaufman had turned the jury against the Rosenbergs with his emotional language.

Over time, 112 judges reviewed the Rosenberg trial. Ninety-six judges agreed with the verdict. Sixteen dissented, not on the merits of the case, but because they questioned legal procedures. Not one said the trial was unfair or that they believed the Rosenbergs were truly innocent and should be pardoned.

THE REACTION

From the beginning, world opinion, especially in Europe, was strongly against the execution of the Rosenbergs. Americans were silent about the sentence for several months. Gradually, their sympathy grew. The Rosenbergs didn't seem so dangerous after all. Ethel's letters from prison seemed like those of a loving wife and mother, not a treacherous spy.

Some sympathetic Americans formed the National Committee to Secure Justice in the Rosenberg Case. They wrote letters to the editors

After they had been convicted and sentenced to die in the electric chair, the Rosenbergs were granted several appeals, due largely to the outpouring of support they received from people around the world. This photograph shows a demonstration on June 18, 1953, in Paris, France, where thousands of supporters called for the pardon of the Rosenbergs. The couple was executed the following day.

of newspapers and magazines. They spoke out in public meetings. Artists and intellectuals joined in the movement, hoping to stop the execution of the Rosenbergs as the appeals continued through the spring of 1953.

Ethel and Julius sent a message to a large rally held on their behalf in New York City. It read:

> We are an ordinary man and wife . . . Like others we spoke for peace, because we did not want our two little sons to live in the shadow of war and death. Like others we spoke for the liberties of our fellow citizens, because we believe, and want our children to believe, in the fine democratic traditions of our country. That is why we are in the death house today . . . there are forces today which hope to silence by death those who speak for peace and democracy . . . And we say to you that no matter what happens to us, you must not be silent.

NO STAY OF EXECUTION

None of the appeals were successful. The Supreme Court turned down the case. By the spring of 1953, it seemed that nothing could stop the execution. New lawyers came into the case with new ideas but fizzled out. President Dwight Eisenhower received some 50,000 letters asking for clemency for the Rosenbergs and then announced he would not interfere in the case.

The executions were set for June 19, 1953. Thousands of Americans from all political viewpoints demonstrated against them. Even people who thought the Rosenbergs were guilty tried to keep them from going to the electric chair. As the day got closer, people around the world—in the Soviet Union, Europe, Mexico, and South America—stood vigil with candles and signs asking for mercy.

June 19 was a Friday. Jewish law states that Jews should not be killed on the Sabbath, so the execution had to take place before sundown,

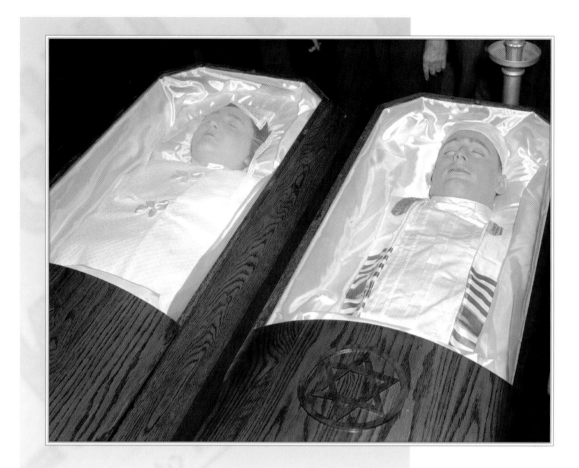

In this photograph taken on June 20, 1953, the day after their executions, the bodies of Ethel and Julius Rosenberg lie in state in a funeral home in Brooklyn, New York. Over 300 supporters were waiting outside the funeral home to pay respects to the couple. Ethel's head was covered with a scrap of silk to hide the portion of her skull that had been shaved for the electrocution helmet. Julius wore a white yarmulke and a prayer shawl.

when the Sabbath began. A rabbi escorted Julius to the electric chair first. After Julius's body was removed, the rabbi took Ethel. Ethel kissed her guard on the cheek and told her good-bye before being strapped into the chair. She died a few minutes later.

Robert Meeropol is shown speaking at a rally for the National Coalition to Abolish the Death Penalty on October 2, 1998. Meeropol is the younger son of Julius and Ethel Rosenberg. After their parents' executions, he and his brother, Michael, were adopted by Abel and Anne Meeropol and lived a relatively normal life. As adults, they wrote the memoir *We Are Your Sons*. Robert is the founder of the Rosenberg Fund for Children, Inc., which provides "for the educational and emotional needs of children whose parents have suffered because of their progressive activities and who, therefore, are no longer able to provide fully for their children," according to the fund's Web site (http://www.rfc.org).

QUESTIONS AND ANSWERS

The Rosenbergs could have saved their lives if they had cooperated with the government and told what they knew about the spy ring. Why didn't they do that? They said they would never betray their friends and if they talked, they'd have to "name names." Many people, however, thought it was because they wanted to be remembered as communist heroes and bring attention to their ideas.

What happened to the other people involved in the case? The Rosenbergs' sons, Michael and Robert, were adopted by a family named Meeropol. They lived privately and no one knew their relationship to the Rosenbergs. As adults, they wrote a book titled *We Are Your Sons*, describing their lives.

David Greenglass spent fifteen years in prison in Pennsylvania, was released, and returned to his family and a quiet life. Morton Sobell served his sentence at Alcatraz Prison in California and later at a federal prison in Atlanta, Georgia. Sobell was released in 1981, still insisting that he was innocent. Many others in the Rosenbergs' circle, who were thought to be spies, disappeared. Joel Barr and Al Savant were later traced to the Soviet Union, where they worked as scientists. Ann Sidorovich was never found. William Perl, another of the CCNY engineers who was accused of spying, was found guilty of perjury and served time in jail.

The FBI files relating to the Rosenberg case were opened to the public in 1977. The files did not offer any new important information; neither did the release in 1995 of Project Verona, a CIA–National Security Agency decoding of secret Soviet reports in the 1940s and 1950s.

It is possible that some questions will never be answered adequately and that the debates about the trial will continue. Ironically, General Leslie Groves, director of the Manhattan Project, told a closed meeting of the Atomic Energy Commission in 1954 that the secrets passed to the Soviets about the atomic bomb were of little value and didn't help them build their own bomb. No one in America would have believed him in 1951, when fear of the Soviet Union overshadowed good judgment.

GLOSSARY

appeal   The transfer of a case from a lower to a higher court for a new hearing.

appellate court   The court that reconsiders a decision made by a lower court; also called the court of appeals.

capital crime   A crime deserving death or calling for the death penalty.

clemency   Mercy.

Communism   A political and economic system whereby goods and property are owned and distributed by the government.

conspiracy   The planning of a crime with others.

courier   Someone who carries messages or goods from one person to another.

deliberations   Discussion and consideration of a case by a jury.

democracy   A political system whereby the people freely elect representatives to the government.

detonate   To set off.

dissent   To disagree.

espionage   Spying for another country.

fission   Splitting or breaking up into parts.

hearsay Evidence based on the reports of others, rather than the personal knowledge of a witness.

incriminate To charge with or show evidence or proof of involvement in a crime.

indictment A formal accusation or charge in the legal process.

objection In law, a challenge to a statement made by the opposing lawyer.

perjury Willfully telling a lie while under oath.

Red Scare A period of general fear of communists.

socialism A political system in which there is collective ownership of goods.

Soviet A council, especially the council form of government under Communism.

FOR MORE INFORMATION

Constitutional Rights Foundation
601 S. Kingsley Drive
Los Angeles CA 90005
(213) 487-5590
Web site: http://crf-usa.org

WEB SITES

Due to the changing nature of Internet links, the Rosen Publishing Group, Inc., has developed an online list of Web sites related to the subject of this book. This site is updated regularly. Please use this link to access the list:

http://www.rosenlinks.com/gttc/tjer/

FOR FURTHER READING

Downing, David. *Communism*. Chicago: Heinemann Library, 2003.

Gonzales, Doreen. *The Manhattan Project and the Atomic Bomb in American History*. Berkeley Heights, NJ: Enslow, 2000.

Krull, Kathleen. *A Kid's Guide to America's Bill of Rights: Curfews, Censorship, and the 100-Pound Giant*. New York: Avon, 1999.

Stein, R. Conrad. *The Manhattan Project*. Chicago: Children's Press, 1993.

Time-Life Books. *Shadow of the Atom, 1950-1960*. (This Fabulous Century). Alexandria, VA: Time-Life Books, 1991.

BIBLIOGRAPHY

Nizer, Louis. *The Implosion Conspiracy*. Garden City, NY: Doubleday, 1973.

Radosh, Ronald, and Joyce Milton. *The Rosenberg Files*. 2nd ed. New Haven, CT: Yale University Press, 1997.

Roberts, Sam. *The Brother: The Untold Story of Atomic Spy David Greenglass and How He Sent His Sister, Ethel Rosenberg, to the Electric Chair*. New York: Random House, 2001.

Sharlitt, Joseph H. *Fatal Error: The Miscarriage of Justice that Sealed the Rosenbergs' Fate*. New York: Scribner, 1989.

PRIMARY SOURCE IMAGE LIST

Cover: Photograph of Ethel and Julius Rosenberg riding to jail. Taken in New York City on March 29, 1951.

Page 4: Photograph of Rosenberg demonstrators at Pennsylvania Station in New York City, taken on June 18, 1953.

Page 6: Photograph of President Harry S Truman at his desk in the White House, Washington, D.C., taken on December 16, 1950.

Page 8: Associated Press photograph of Soviets discovering a tunnel in Berlin, Germany, filled with surveillance equipment, taken on April 24, 1956.

Page 9: Photograph of Dr. Klaus Fuchs leaving Heathrow Airport in London, England in 1959.

Page 10: Photographs of Anatoli Yakovlev, Julius Rosenberg, Harry Gold, Morton Sobell, David Greenglass, and Klaus Fuchs. Housed in the National Archives Record Administration.

Page 12: Photograph of Julius and Ethel Rosenberg.

Page 14: Photograph of Robert and Michael Rosenberg, taken on June 10, 1953, in Washington, D.C.

Page 15: Photograph of socialist rally in Madison Square Garden, New York City, taken on November 3, 1932.

Page 17: Photograph mug shot of Julius Rosenberg, taken on July 20, 1950, in New York City.

Page 18: Photograph of Julius Rosenberg being escorted into FBI building, taken on July 17, 1950. Inset: Photographic portrait of Morton Sobell, housed in the U.S. National Archives.

Page 22: Photograph of Rosenberg trial jury, taken outside Federal Court in New York City on March 29, 1951.

Page 25: Photograph of an atomic bomb test in Yucca Flat, Nevada, taken on February 18, 1955.

Page 27: Government exhibit 2, sketch of high explosive lens mold from the atomic bomb. Government exhibit 8, sketch of cross section of atomic bomb. Sketch of setup to implode tubular materials, government exhibit 7. All drawn by David Greenglass. From the Julius and Ethel Rosenberg Case File, 1951. Housed in the National Archives Record Administration.

Page 29: Photograph of nuclear explosion. Taken over the Bikini Atoll on March 27, 1954.

Page 30: Photograph of nuclear fallout shelter in New York City, photographed on May 19, 1955.

Page 32: Photograph of Irving Saypol, Myles Lane, and Roy Cohn, taken in New York City on April 19, 1950.

Page 34: Photograph of David and Ruth Greenglass, government exhibit 13 from the Julius and Ethel Rosenberg Case File, 1951. Housed in the National Archives Record Administration.

Page 35: Photograph of Mike and Ann Sidorovich, government exhibit 3 from the Julius and Ethel Rosenberg Case File, 1951. Housed in the National Archives Record Administration.

Page 36: Photograph of Jell-O box, imitation raspberry flavor, government exhibit 33 from the Julius and Ethel Rosenberg Case File, 1951. Housed in the National Archives Record Administration.

Page 37: Photograph of government exhibit 10, brown paper wrapper which contained $4000 that Julius Rosenberg gave to David Greenglass. Photograph of government exhibit 24a and 24b, airline tickets and passenger manifests. Photostat of a picture of a console table, government exhibit 28. Bank deposit slip and ledger from June 4, 1945, government exhibit 17. All from the Julius and Ethel Rosenberg Case File, 1951. Housed in the National Archives Record Administration.

Page 38: Photograph of Harry Gold testifying at open hearing in Washington, D.C., on April 26, 1956.

Page 41: Photograph of John Finerty, Malcolm Sharp, Emanuel Bloch, Fyke Farmer, and Daniel Marshall, taken on June 19, 1953, in Washington, D.C.

Page 43: Associated Press photograph of Julius and Ethel Rosenberg, taken in 1951 in New York City.

Page 47: Associated Press photograph of Ethel Rosenberg arriving at Sing Sing prison, taken in Ossining, New York, on April 11, 1951.

Page 48: Photograph of Morton Sobell transferring to Alcatraz Prison, taken in 1952.

Page 51: Photograph of a rally on behalf of the Rosenbergs, taken in Paris, France, on June 18, 1953.

Page 53: Photograph of Ethel and Julius Rosenberg lying in state, taken in Brooklyn, New York, on June 20, 1953.

Page 54: Associated Press photograph of Robert Meeropol, taken in St. Louis, Missouri, on October 2, 1998.

INDEX

ABOUT THE AUTHOR

Betty Burnett is a former newspaper reporter who has written fifteen books. She lives in St. Louis, Missouri.

CREDITS

Cover, pp. 1, 8, 43, 54 © AP/Wide World Photos; pp. 4, 14, 15, 18 (inset) 22, 30, 32, 38, 41, 47, 48, 53 © Bettmann/Corbis; pp. 6, 10, 27, 34, 35, 36, 37, U.S. National Archives and Records Administration; pp. 9, 17, 18 (top), 51 © Hulton/Archive/Getty Images; pp. 12, 25, 29 © Corbis.

Series Design and Layout: Les Kanturek; **Editor:** Christine Poolos

DATE DUE